CONTENTS

1 Introduction   3

2 First Observation: *Bee* Who You Were Born to Be   5

3 Second Observation: Work Hard and *Bee* Creative   11

4 Third Observation: Appreciate Your Community   16

5 Fourth Observation: You Will *Bee* Stung   21

6 Fifth Observation: Celebrate All Abundance   26

7 Sixth Observation: Stop to Smell the Flowers   31

8 Seventh Observation: Recognize Your Value   35

9 Eighth Observation: Learn to Live With Drones   39

10 Ninth Observation: *Bee* Happy   44

ACKNOWLEDGMENTS

The pictures were taken by Dr. Shanon Sterringer, Maria Sterringer, and Rev. Peter Mihalic.
The hives were built by Richard Sterringer.
The inspiration came from St. Hildegard of Bingen.

The bees are a gift from God.

INTRODUCTION

My desire to become a beekeeper began to surface over a decade ago when I experienced an unusual occurrence. I was sitting in my room and all of a sudden the ceiling light fixture above me was full of bees. I had no idea where they came from or how they got in the light fixture, but as quickly as they came they were gone. For a moment I thought I had imagined it because it was such an odd experience. It is possible they were swarming and looking for a new home or, as I wanted to believe, maybe they were calling me to become a beekeeper. I have heard it said that beekeepers do not choose bees - bees choose beekeepers. However the bees came to be in my ceiling fixture that evening, they sparked something within me that continued to stir.

Over the next few years I found myself on a number of occasions thinking about the possibility of caring for my own hives. I knew it was time when we moved back to Fairport Harbor in the Spring of 2016. The property we had purchased, which is now The HILDEGARDEN, had previously had a situation with honeybees (although in that instance the bees had formed their hive in the wall obstructing the air-conditioning unit). I felt that not only did the bees belong here at The HILDEGARDEN, but that there were some valuable lessons to be learned from them.

I had never been stung by a bee and was a bit scared of what that would feel like, yet I felt it just might be worth the pain. Having been stung many times now, I can say it is. Though maybe the bees would not agree... My time with the bees this past summer has been truly transforming. I have in fact learned some very valuable life lessons from observing them. As I thought about my observations many wise words from St. Hildegard came to mind.

This book has been inspired to be a tool for spiritual growth. It is not a resource for beekeeping. I am in no way a professional beekeeper. I am a Catholic minister and a new Bee Mama in love with God, life, and my girls.

Who is Hildegard and why is she at the hive?
Hildegard of Bingen was a 12th century German Mystic, recently named a Saint and Doctor in the Roman Catholic Church. In her 81 years of life, Hildegard sought to grow in relationship with God and all of the created world through a theological concept she called *viriditas*. The idea of *viriditas* provided Hildegard with a language and image to describe the life-source inherent in every part of the created world – from human beings down to honeybees and even inanimate objects including plants and stones. Hildegard left us an enormous amount of writing describing the nature of creation, divine order, spirituality, and holistic health. It is through her inspiration that this personal reflection on the spirituality of bees was born.

In 2016 I earned a Ph.D. in Ethical and Creative Leadership using the works of Hildegard. As part of my research, The HILDEGARDEN was formed in Fairport Harbor, Ohio. It is here in this sacred place that the honeybees used in this reflective work have found their home.

Newly assembled hives in The HILDEGARDEN basement.

First Observation: *Bee* Who You Were Created to Be

Brood cells – the white flecks are newly laid eggs.

Every bee begins its journey in the world in the same way. An egg is planted in a cell by the queen. At this initial stage all eggs are exactly the same. The egg develops into different roles - a queen, a drone, or a worker bee - based on the size of the cell, the amount of royal jelly fed, and the intent of the hive. Bees are either born as a queen (rare), male drones (very few in relation to the worker bees), or female workers (thousands per day in healthy hives). Among the workers there are particular roles – some are given the task of caring for the developing eggs, many are sent out to forage bringing back pollen and nectar, some are responsible for honey production, and a few are in charge of clean-up and hive protection. As in any civilized society, there are many different roles to be filled and the bees decide collectively who will assume various roles. The way in which the bees communicate these decisions through vibration and dance is astounding.

In the beginning chapters of her work, *Book of Divine* Works, Hildegard of Bingen wrote, "With Wisdom God has rightly put the universe in order," and this is certainly evident when one observes the inner-workings of egg laying and production within a honey bee hive.

It may seem unfair that a bee formed into a worker bee has no possible path to being a queen. Or that one is born a drone with seemingly little role to play in the overall development of the hive if he has not been chosen to impregnate the queen. Some may even say this natural order reflects something of a "caste system" which is not positively embraced in a democratic culture. There are instances where worker bees assume the role of laying eggs, and therefore drones impregnate females other than the queen, and the end result is always discord and even chaos within the hive.

The queen is marked with a white dot on her forward.

Under normal circumstances there is only one queen per hive. Her role is unique and critical to the overall health and wellbeing of the hive. However, just as important as her role is the role of every other bee. For a hive to be healthy, every bee must be willing to embrace the role she (and in a few instances he) was created for and to function as fully in that role as possible. The role of the queen may seem privileged to some, but even her role is marked with pain, suffering, and uncertainty.

What lesson can we take from observing the bees in this way? Each one of us is created equal in dignity and purpose to everyone else. Like it or not, there is a natural hierarchy of roles in place in the created world. Some of us are born into situations of privilege and abundance (fed a bit more royal jelly if you will) while others are born into situations that are obviously difficult and filled with obstacles and suffering. The paths we are called to walk may seem quite different. Yet, we each begin in exactly the same way – a spark of divine light formed and fashioned for a purpose. In our own individual way we are created to contribute something to the whole.

We are born into a community to bring light, love, and goodness to the whole. Each one of us comes into this world with particular purpose. Hildegard fully understood that we are created within an ordered universe. This is not a reference to gender, sexual orientation, or culturally defined roles. It is a reference to each one of us having been created for a unique vocation. We come into this world as "light-bearers" called to bring light into any place we experience darkness. The path we desire to walk may at times be motivated by ambition, money, power, comfort, or even self-recognition. In many of these situations we find ourselves waking up to the fact that we are on a path that is not in tune with our divine call. This is not to say that our divinely ordered path will not be lined with abundant gifts of every kind; certainly that is possible, but seeking abundance as our end goal can distract us from the path. Identifying and overcoming our ego-self within the discernment process is the most challenging obstacle a seeker must face. Our ego, not our inner light, often dictates where we go, or try to go, and that can cause an enormous amount of discord within our families, workplace, and within ourselves. Letting go of our ego in order to discover our divine self will provide the nourishment needed to produce much fruit, or in the case of the honey bees, it provides the necessary elements to produce rich and abundant honey.

Hildegard at the Hive

"The Living Light which reveals miracles says: Watch over that garden which the divine gift has planted, and take care that its herbs do not wither…Do not overshadow your garden with the weariness of silence, but in the True Light weed out those things which must be weeded out with discretion. Illuminate your temple with benevolence, and burn incense in your censer, so that its smoke may ascend to the palace of the living God. And you will live forever." Letter 36 to Hermann, Bishop of Constance

Reflection Questions

1) Who am I really? Do I truly know myself or do I identify exclusively with my titles, accomplishments, or labels attached by others?

2) Do I feel content with where I am at in life right now?

3) What is really motivating my actions?

4) Do I believe God has ordered everything in the universe as Hildegard stated in the *Book of Divine Works*?

5) Do I radiate peace, joy, and acceptance or am I anxious, angry, and jealous of others?

6) Is my life harmonious or filled with discord?

7) What lesson can I personally take from the way in which the bees cooperate in community?

Journaling Page

_____

_____

_____

_____

_____

_____

_____

_____

_____

_____

_____

_____

_____

Second Observation: Work Hard and *Bee* Creative

Inspection of early spring honey comb.

There is hardly a creature to be found that works as diligently and creatively as the honey bee. It is estimated that a foraging bee must visit 2 million flowers to produce one pound of honey. These girls work hard. As soon as the sun begins to warm the door of the hive the bees begin to emerge soaking in the morning sun in preparation for the day's work which, when the circumstances are right, will produce a plethora of pollen and nectar for the hive. In addition to nourishing the bees, a healthy environment helps to produce beautiful golden honey.

How exactly is honey produced? Honey is produced when foraging bees gather nectar from flowers and ingest it. This nectar mixes with the proteins and enzymes in the stomach of the bee and is regurgitated into a honeycomb cell. This process make take place several times, among a number of bees, until the process is complete. Once in the honeycomb cell the bees will dry out any extra moisture by fanning their wings and creating "caps" on the honeycomb. This preserves the honey for later use.

This honeybee did not want to stop working!

Not only do the bees produce honey, but they also produce royal jelly. This is produced by the glands at the top of a nursing bee's head. The amount of royal jelly fed to the developing egg/larvae, coupled with the size of the cell, determines what type of bee will develop. Queens are fed a diet exclusively of royal jelly. Drones and worker bees are fed special formulas providing the necessary nutrients for their development.

How is the comb made? Bees also produce wax, which in essence is "bee sweat" deposited from the abdomen to form perfect hexagon shapes. Why hexagons? Because they are the most efficient use of wax allowing the bees to produce more comb with less materials. They reflect perfect symmetry, some would say "sacred mathematics," providing an example of God's ever-present fingerprint in every part of the created world.

Bees need the greenness of nature to do their work. When we contaminate our earth with chemicals, including spraying in the spring for dandelions and other weeds, we directly impact the quality of life for the honey bee. Without the work of the honey bee, human beings would not be able to survive. While doing the work necessary to sustain themselves, the bees pollinate approximately 75% of the food supply for human beings. It has been suggested that human beings could only survive a few years if honey bees were to become extinct. The small honeybee truly "rules the world" though her work is largely unnoticed and unappreciated.

Hildegard at the Hive

"Without the WORD of God no creature has being. God's WORD is in all creation, visible and invisible. The WORD is living, being, spirit, all verdant greening, all creativity. All creation is awakened, called, by the resounding melody, God's invocation of the WORD. This WORD manifests in every creature." Symphonia.

A piece of comb that broke off from the hive.

Reflection Questions

1) Do I feel I am engaged in meaningful work? Or do I just "punch a time-clock" each day?

2) Do I feel my job reflects my inner passion?

3) If I could do any type of work, would it be the work I am currently engaged in or would I choose something else?

4) Am I aware of how my lifestyle choices effect other people's experience of work? For example, do I ever consider inquiring into the labor practices or commercial trade agreements of companies I support?

5) Am I concerned with environmental sustainability or do I use without concern for the eco-footprint I might be leaving?

6) What lesson can I personally take from the way in which the bees engage in work?

Journaling Page

_____

_____

_____

_____

_____

_____

_____

_____

_____

_____

_____

_____

Third Observation: Appreciate Your Community

Honeybees cannot normally survive outside of the hive. They need to be a part of the community. Bees that either get lost or are exiled from the hive will not last very long. Some may attempt to find a home in another hive, but often times they are rejected as an intruder.

Why would a bee be exiled from the hive? One example is when a hive is in need of a new queen it may produce two or more queens in an effort to restore order. Once the queens emerge it is understood (except in an African Killer Bee hive) that there can only be one queen per hive, if it is a healthy hive. Dueling queens will either fight until one remains or one will be exiled from the hive. The same is true with drones.

Drones are male bees and they do not work. They are bred to impregnate the queen. When winter approaches they drones are considered a drain on the food supply and since they do not work they are not an efficient part of the whole. The female bees will either kill the drones or will simply run them out of the hive. Because drones are unable to find their own food, separated from the community they will certainly perish.

When the community begins to become overcrowded the bees do something remarkable. They gather together, with their queen, possibly a new queen, and they swarm. A swarm of bees is a docile gathering, yet it tends to incite fear. When bees swarm they are simply setting out, as a community, to find a new home. Approximately two-thirds of the hive swarms while one-third stays back. A beekeeper can often tell when the bees are preparing to swarm by the queen cells that are produced. Interestingly, the queen that leaves the hive with the swarm has no input into where the new home will be. The bees gather in a convenient place, often on a tree branch, while a few scouts head out in search of a possible place to relocate. Each of the scouts shares the information and as a community the bees decide which location would best fit their needs. The way in which a swarm relocates in community is truly a miracle of nature.

In much the same way as the honeybee, we too are called to live in community with one another. There is a lot we can learn from the way in which the swarm decides collectively where they will relocate. It is not the decision of one person, or even one "special interest" group, but the decision is made by taking into consideration the common good of the entire hive.

Understanding our call to participate in community is fundamental to who we are as human beings. While there will always be those members that we would like to "exile" from our midst, in reality we need to find ways to work together. They too are a part of the whole and for us to truly heal as a nation, society, and global world acceptance of and appreciation for the great gift of our community is necessary.

Hildegard at the Hive
"I, the highest and fiery power, have kindled every spark of life... I decide on all reality. With my lofty wings I fly above the globe... With every breeze, as with invisible life that contains everything. I awaken everything to life... I am life, whole and entire."
Book of Divine Works, Vision 1:2

Reflection Questions

1) In what ways do I feel called to be a part of the community in which I live, work, or worship?

2) Do I recognize my interconnectedness with God and others?

3) Have I experienced a miracle of nature?

4) Using the example of the honeybees, do I feel as though I am an active part of my hive? Or have I been feeling as though I have been marginalized from the inner hive?

5) What do I love most about my community? What do I least like about it?

6) How can I be an agent of change within my community?

An inspection of the overall well-being of the community in this hive.

Journaling Page

_____

_____

_____

_____

_____

_____

_____

_____

_____

_____

_____

_____

_____

Fourth Observation: You Will Get Stung

.

It has been said that any beekeeper who claims s/he has never been stung is most likely not a beekeeper. It does not matter how much protection one wears, if you decide you are called to be a beekeeper, at some point in your journey you will be stung and it hurts. My first summer as a beekeeper I wore hats, nets, gloves, jackets, and suits and was stung well over a dozen times. Each time I realized that being stung is part of the experience. Assuming one is not allergic to the sting, the beekeeper will recover, of course not without some irritating swelling and itching, but nonetheless will recover. The honeybee, on the other hand, will not. When a honey bee stings she dies.

Innately all creatures want to live and so the choice to sting is made only when the honeybee feels threatened or called to protect the hive. When a honeybee stings she has willingly sacrificed herself for what she perceives as the greater good. She has given the gift of herself in service of her community.

A sting incurred by a beekeeper is not normally the result of a violent attack (unless of course one is dealing with an "attitude hive" but those are uncommon), but rather should be viewed as an act of love on behalf of the bee towards her community.

Interaction with others – human, animal, and even bees – creates situations that can be hurtful. We may feel that by protecting ourselves we are immune, but in reality we are inevitably going to get hurt in one way or another. It is a part of our lived experience. When we love others we make ourselves vulnerable. The challenge is to keep loving, keep trusting, keep beekeeping, as though we have never been stung.

Rick Sterringer watering the bees ☺

Hildegard at the Hive

"I see that there is darkness in some part of you. Why do I say this? Because your heart is bound up in that sadness which is encircled by doubt, like a millstone questioning, "what is my purpose? What sort of purpose do I have? Now, you should take

note of the day which arises in the morning with a bright dawn , but which afterward, is racked by shifting storms. Such is your life. For if you always had prosperity, you would be like that crab that cannot walk straight... God established the sun to give light to the whole earth and to dispel darkness... So do not fear those things that torment you."

Letter to Prelate 146r

A beautiful frame of honey partially capped.

Reflection Questions

1) Am I carrying a hurt or "sting" from the past that I wish would heal?

2) Who hurt me? Why did s/he hurt me?

3) Has that incident created an obstacle in my discernment process?

4) Am I ready to forgive that person, even if s/he is not sorry for the pain caused?

5) In what ways have I been called to sacrifice my well-being for others? How do I feel about that?

6) What lesson can I take from the way in which the honeybee offers the gift of herself for the overall benefit of the hive?

Journaling Page

_____

_____

_____

_____

_____

_____

_____

_____

_____

_____

_____

Fifth Observation: Celebrate Your Abundance

Honeybees need very little to produce abundantly: water, flowers, sunlight, and a home. With those basic elements honeybees are able to produces pounds of beautiful, glistening honey. In ancient times honey was viewed as sacred, a food of the gods. Many Egyptian kings and queens were buried with vats of honey to feed them in the afterlife. Honey is the only known food that never spoils. Honey will last indefinitely.

While honeybees do not share the gift of their abundance knowingly (and at times may sting to protect their honey from being robbed), they continue to produce with the intention of sharing. Worker bees only live 30-60 days. This means that they may never get to enjoy the product they have produced. They make honey for those who will need its nourishment after they are gone. Honeybees labor for others.

Receiving the gift of honey calls us to remember the amount of labor and creativity that went into its production. It is most appropriate for the beekeeper to give thanks, not only to God but also to the bees, for their labor of love. Light breeds light and when we recognize the light present in something as simple (and complex) as the honeybee, we become vessels of light.

The bees teach us that the greatest gift we can give another is the gift of ourselves. Each one of us is born with unique gifts and talents. Each and every one of us is divine. When we use our divinely given gifts for others we create a world filled with love and light. Transformation of our world will only become a reality when we surrender our own will in service of others.

Observing the honeybees flitter around on a warm, sunny day, celebrating their abundant life can be a spiritual experience. It calls the observer to take notice of her/his own blessings. To give thanks for the things in life we often take for granted – water, flowers, sunlight, and a home.

Hildegard at the Hive

"Almighty God, who founded the universe, has revealed wondrous deeds under various signs. God, who is wonderful in gifts, has distributed them to each and every creature in accord with divine will... God's deeds are established in such a way that no creature remains so incomplete as to lack anything in its nature. Instead, each creature possesses the fullness of all that is perfect and useful. And thus everything emanating from Wisdom lives in it like a pure and uniquely beautiful jewel and gleams in the purest brilliance of its being."

Book of Divine Works, Vision 9:2

Reflection Questions

1) What am I thankful for today?

2) What blessings in my life do I tend to take for granted?

3) How can I come to more fully recognize the abundant gifts I have been given?

4) Do I tend to be concerned with a lack of temporal things or am I focused on the gifts that last forever?

5) What lesson can I take from the way in which the honeybee continues to produce honey, even though she may not get to enjoy the product of her labor?

Two beautiful honey frames.

Journaling Page

_____

_____

_____

_____

_____

_____

_____

_____

_____

_____

_____

Sixth Observation: Stop to Smell the Flowers

A beautiful shot taken by my daughter Maria Sterringer.

One of the most valuable lessons we can learn from the honeybee is to take time to stop and smell, look at, photograph, and appreciate, the flowers. It takes thousands of flowers to produce a very small amount of honey. This includes flowers that do not normally appeal to us, such as the spring dandelions, which are of great importance to the honeybee. And they should be of importance to us. Dandelions are considered a "nutrient-powerhouse" for human beings. The flowers as well as the greens can be consumed in a number of ways for optimum health benefits. Yet, we tend to look at them as little more than a pesky weed cluttering our lawn. When we spray our lawns with chemicals or rip out wild flower beds, we are starving the very creatures who feed us.

Coming to recognize our integral relationship with creation calls us to be conscious of the great web of life. If the bees are to feed us, we need to feed the bees. The bees teach us to look at creation through a new lens. A lens focused on integral relationship. How often do we really stop and notice the beauty all around us? We race from one place to the next, usually in our cars, failing to notice God's abounding grace all around us. We live in a beautiful world and it is speaking to us, if only we could slow down to listen.

Hildegard of Bingen wrote many letters on the inherent fingerprint of God in the natural world. Her theological concept of *viriditas* calls us to grow in awareness that the same life force that animates plants, flowers, honeybees also animates human beings. We all come from, and return to, the same Creator / Source.

Hildegard at the Hive

"Then God created us in the light of divine power. God placed us in the inextinguishable day of Paradise which, without decay, was to live in fruitfulness... God is the living light in every respect. From God all light shines. Therefore, we remain a light that gives off life through God. For we are fire according to our essence."
Book of Divine Works, Vision 5:15

This comb was built in a place in the hive that was problematic. Before removing it I wanted to preserve its beauty in a photo.

Reflection Questions

1) Do I take time out each day to appreciate the diversity of life all around me?

2) In what ways have I experienced a sacred presence in the natural world?

3) Do I feel as though I am full of *viriditas* (greening power) or have I been in a dry spell?

4) What obstacles / beliefs keep me from opening myself up to a more intimate relationship with all of creation?

5) Do I take time each day to look for "God-moments"?

6) What activities or attitudes are weighing me down each day preventing me from appreciating the simple gifts?

Bees hanging out at the hive.

Journaling Page

_____

_____

_____

_____

_____

_____

_____

_____

_____

_____

_____

_____

Seventh Observation: Recognize Your Value

Two bees hanging out on the roof.

Until recently the value of an individual honeybee was not fully recognized or appreciated. We have created a context in which we have almost fully annihilated the honeybee pushing it towards near extinction. A single hive can easily hold upwards of 50,000 honeybees. Though they may seem insignificant, all share in equal value and dignity. It does not take long to go from losing a "few honeybees" to a total hive collapse. Treating each and every beautiful bee as though she (and he) is a reflection of some aspect of God, changes the way in which we view the whole.

Honeybees have been feared, exterminated, swatted at, and avoided. It has been rare, at least until recently, that they are celebrated, appreciated, invited, or embraced as necessary to our environment. Unfortunately, the resurgence in interest in the honeybee has not emerged because of desire to love or care for God's smallest creature, but largely because we are feeling the devastating consequences of not protecting honeybees. Why are we so afraid of them? Yes, they sting and so we have labeled them undesirable creatures. Without taking the time to get to know and understand the divine nature of a honeybee, we decided they were not valuable, even disposable, and have almost pushed them to a point of extinction.

We do the same thing with people. Consciously or

subconsciously we assign a higher value to certain people that we equate with greatness. And we treat others as though they are disposable. We assume those who hold power, money, and offices must be more important than those who are living "ordinary" lives. And we assign even a lower value to those we deem "undesirable" or different. Just as in the case of the honeybee, those who seem least important, most disposable to our society, are often invaluable to our daily existence. We fail to protect the most vulnerable in our midst from harm.

Hildegard at the Hive

"The True Light says these words: There was a flower in a certain valley, but the gardeners came and planted a thorny hedge all around it, and so, in their malice, choked it off, with the leaves all bent down, and broken up by the winds. Thus that flower lost all its vitality. And still the gardeners paid no attention to it and did not love it. Instead, they went looking for another flower, but, finding only a weed, they cast it aside. Then, they found a delicate, red flower, and turned their thoughts wholly to it. Nevertheless, they did not protect it. Yet a certain man came along, and set a protective covering over that flower, so that it would not utterly perish." Letter 365

Reflection Questions

1) Who in my life, or in society, have I deemed insignificant or disposable? On what grounds have I made that determination?

2) Was there a time/or times, when you have felt insignificant in relation to others? What influenced my feelings?

3) Think of a time when you felt really good about a contribution you made or an accomplishment you celebrated. What was it about the experience that made you feel good? How do you feel about it now?

4) What lessons can we draw from the mistakes we have made in the way we have treated honeybees?

A worker bee carrying a dead bee out of the hive.

Journaling Page

_____

_____

_____

_____

_____

_____

_____

_____

_____

_____

_____

_____

Eighth Observation: Learn to Live With Drones

The bee in the center is a drone. Notice the difference in shape.

One cannot observe the honeybee without acknowledging "the elephant" (or maybe more appropriate to say "the drone") in the room. Honeybees are a matriarchal, female dominated society. The queen, as well as all of the workers, are female. There are a number of male bees (drones) in each hive, yet they do not work, they cannot forage, they do not even sting. They are bred for one purpose – to impregnate the queen. That act results in the drone's death. The other drones are allowed to live in the hive for much of the summer months, but are usually terminated or exiled from the hive before the winter because they are a drain on the limited food supply. Drones are also responsible for attracting to the hive the dreaded Varroa Mite. Other than producing baby bees, and infecting the hive with mites, what benefits do the drones bring to the hive? Not too much (sorry guys).

How then can observing the honeybees relationship with the drones help us to grow in light and love? Though the worker bees do not benefit from the drones, they learn to live with them. The worker bees provide nursing care for the developing drones, food and shelter for the mature drones, and a community where all live in harmony as co-members of the hive (at least until winter approaches!)

What lesson can we draw from this? Men and women, gay and straight, young and old, black and white, rich and poor, etc. and etc. – we are all called to live together in mutual respect, love, and light. There may be times when collaboration and understanding seems impossible (and maybe even times when terminating or exiling someone seems like an attractive option!); however, with a concentrated effort there are always creative solutions to be found. Solutions which create healthy, light-bearing relationships that can withstand even the harshest winter months!

A frame with drone cells. They are larger than worker bee cells.

Hildegard at the Hive

"He who is about to come will purge all things, and He will re-create them in a different way, and He will wash away all the blemishes of the times and the seasons, and He will make all things ever new."

Letter15r

I could not resist including this picture.   These are two of my dearest friends, Fr. Pete Mihalic and Bishop Prasad Gallela. They are ordained men laboring ceaselessly for the Kingdom of God. They are "worker bees" in every aspect, yet they are male and so in the world of honeybees they would be considered drones and would not survive the winter ☺

Reflection Questions

1) How well do I respect or even attempt to understand members of the opposite sex? Members of another faith tradition? Members of a different social or cultural context?

2) Do I make assumptions regarding men/women that leads to tension and division?

3) In what ways do I need to improve the way in which I engage in relationship with people I consider different from myself?

4) Are there things I can do to make "living with" others more pleasant and joyful?

A lone drone hanging on a stick.

Journaling Page

_____

_____

_____

_____

_____

_____

_____

_____

_____

_____

_____

_____

Ninth Observation: *Bee* Happy!

The most valuable lesson I have learned during these last few months observing the honeybees is to find creative ways to *bee* happy! Life is too short, and too awesome, to be anything other than happy. Yes, our lives are filled with pain and suffering, yet in the midst of that there is much beauty and joy – focus on the light and happiness will follow!

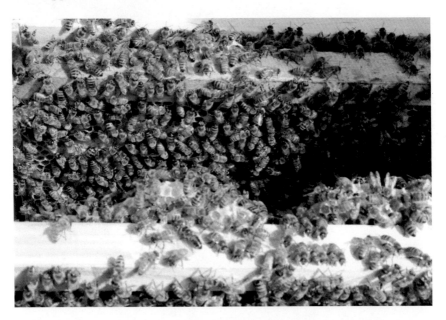

We waste too much valuable time wishing we were something or someone else. It has been said, "It is good to be king / queen" but is it really? The life of the honeybee queen is not all it appears to be. After she is impregnated by 10-12 drones she spends the rest of her days laying 1,000 or more eggs per day (many times her own body weight). She does not get out often and does little more than lay eggs. The worker bees on the other hand get to see the world, enjoy the sunshine, care for the young, and plan for the future. The well-being of the hive depends not only the vitality of the queen, but equally on the happiness of the workers.

Happiness is not a feeling or a moment; it is a state of being. Happiness is being in harmony with all of creation. It is not something that can be bought or acquired from others. It is internal and results when we do the following:

1) Journey within to discover who you are and be the person you were born to be.

2) Work hard, in whatever role or state of life you find yourself, and be creative in your efforts.

3) Appreciate the great gift of community. We were not created to be alone. We were created to be in relationship.

4) Be prepared to be hurt. Anyone who claims s/he has never been hurt has never loved.

5) Recognize and celebrate abundance in your life, even if it surfaces in a form different from what you expected. We are often "rich" in ways that have nothing to do with money or material goods.

6) Take time to stop and smell the flowers – and maybe draw, photograph, or simply give thanks for their beauty and resilience.

7) Recognize your value. You are created in the image and likeness of God. You are born to be light for our world. You are invaluable.

8) Learn to live with drones. This means learning to live with everyone who is different from you. Make an effort to grow in your understanding and acceptance of others.

9) And when you have mastered all of the above you will find it is very easy to *BEE* HAPPY!

Hildegard at the Hive

*"In a spiritual vision of my soul, I saw and heard these words:
O sons of Love, you who have drunk from that sparkling,
inexhaustible fountain, and who have been enkindled by that
inextinguishable lamp... May the purest light of the true sun
illumine you, and may it teach you to persevere in the holy ways of
life to a happy end so that you may live in eternity in true bliss."*

Letter to the Monk Guibert, 109r

Reflection Questions

1) How do I define happiness?

2) Which of the above lessons do I need to work on?

3) Do I tend to allow negative energy to rule my day?

4) How can I maintain an element of happiness and joy in the midst of a "bad" day?

5) Today I am happy because…

Journaling Page

_____

_____

_____

_____

_____

_____

_____

_____

_____

_____

_____

_____

ABOUT THE AUTHOR

Dr. Shanon Sterringer has been a Roman Catholic minister in the
Diocese of Cleveland, Ohio for almost two decades. She has a MA
in Theology from St. Mary's Seminary and Graduate School of
Theology in Wickliffe, Ohio; a MA in Ministry from Ursuline
College in Pepperpike, Ohio; a D.Min in the topic of Women's
Leadership in the Roman Catholic Church from St. Mary's
Seminary and Graduate School of Theology in Wickliffe, Ohio;
and a Ph.D. in Ethical and Creative Leadership using the example
of St. Hildegard of Bingen, Doctor of the Church from Union
Institute & University in Cincinnati, Ohio. She has recently
published part of her dissertation in a book entitled, *An Enchanted
Journey.* Shanon has been married for 26 years and has 3 beautiful
daughters. Recently she and her family purchased a closed
Byzantine Catholic Church and converted it into a non-
denominational spiritual center, The HILDEGARDEN.
She now lives on the property with her family and approximately
100,000 honeybees.